"When good Americans die,
they go to Paris."

Oscar Wilde

34060685R00052

Made in the USA
Lexington, KY
18 March 2019